Minnesota

on my mind

FALCON®

Design, typesetting, and other prepress work by
Falcon®, Helena, Montana. Printed in Korea.

Library of Congress Number: 889-080765

ISBN 0-937959-70-7

Front cover photos
T. RUMREICH/FROZEN IMAGES *sunrise at Silver Island Lake*
DANIEL J. COX *common loon*

Back cover photos
CRAIG BLACKLOCK *fall colors on Oberg Mountain*
ANNIE GRIFFITHS BELT *stacking hay*
DANIEL J. COX *whitetail fawn*

For extra copies of this book
please check with your local bookstore, or write to
Falcon, P.O. Box 1718, Helena, MT 59624
or call toll-free 1-800-582-2665

FALCON®

A great blue heron at sundown   JIM BRANDENBURG/FROZEN IMAGES

introduction

There are, of course, many Minnesotas. The one I grew up in is flat and rural, sparsely populated, generally treeless. It is dedicated mile after mile to the production of row crops in regular square and rectangular patches. From the air it looks as complicated and interesting as a fine quilt, but most people passing through it on the ground will say that it is extremely monotonous.

When I was eighteen, I climbed into my maroon and white Chrysler and headed for The Cities (which are, as every Minnesotan knows, Minneapolis and St. Paul), delirious to be out on my own at last, and quite certain that I had left the prairies forever. This seemed confirmed as fact when I abandoned Minnesota four years later for a job on Capitol Hill. But in eleven months I was home again and five years after that I had returned to the Minnesota countryside, to the corn and bean country, as happy to be returning as I had been to leave.

I suppose that strangers passing through my part of Minnesota, which is beautiful in its own peculiar way, must remark as I often have on passing through some strange and forlorn place, "Why here! Why on earth would somebody who had crossed the Atlantic and caught a train and then an ox-drawn wagon, who had endured every kind of privation, who had risked life and limb to make a better start, why in the *world* would such a person decide that *this* was the place to settle?" Who can say? I myself roam the United States, falling in love with place after place. I love indiscriminately ocean shores and mountaintops and sand dunes and the Sonoran desert and mangrove swamps and cypress swamps and badlands and deep canyons and rivers and river flats and any place with rocks and crowded city centers. I come to almost any place and I think, "Oh, yes, this is it. I would like to live here. I know I could be very happy here." No practical consideration constrains me from moving to one of them. But I don't move. I stay right where I am, and most of the time I am convinced that I have done the right thing. Who can say what mysterious threads bind us to a particular place?

I think that place is imprinted upon us when we are very young in the same way that a gosling settles on the first potential parent that comes along, and that ever after, whatever rebellions we might make against it, we carry with us its memory, measuring all others against it. The biologist Edward O. Wilson argues in *Biophilia*, in fact, that this imprinting is in some way inscribed in our genes. The world over, he remarks, people who wish to make an extravagantly beautiful place come down to the same pattern: a pool of water or a stream, a grassy knoll, a scattering of tall, shade-bearing trees. They recreate the landscape of the savanna, in which our species emerged as distinctly human. Wilson says we carry with us as a birthright the memory of that ideal first place.

This sounds true to me, although I couldn't begin to prove it. What seems to me demonstrably true, however, is that familiarity with a place breeds love of it. There is no place so desolate and unyielding that it does not have at some time of the day or year in some light or weather its own distinct and absolute beauty. The farm I grew up on, for example, was not even particularly rewarding as agricultural land. A third of it was a hilly waste and the rest was rather rocky and thin by the lavish standards of Minnesota farmland. The buildings on it had seen much better days. They were approached along a narrow, dusty township road lined on either side by a rank growth of weeds. The well served also as a hibernaculum for the local population of garter snakes. To fetch a pail of water at certain times of spring or fall involved picking your barefooted way through a gauntlet of snakes.

Yet, I remember this place, not romantically, as lovely. In every season of the year it afforded

Paddling into the dusk   R. HAMILTON SMITH

fine views of the setting sun across the bluffs of the Chippewa River. There was a meadow lush with wild strawberries in the springtime and bursting with wildflowers in the summer. There was a little pond on which the winter skating was fine. At the far corner of the pasture stood a magnificent black walnut tree so wide of limb that you could nap on it in the shade of a lazy summer day. There were two springs that gurgled and sang the year around. Even the dusty township lane had its allure on still nights in the full moon. I would walk it alone in the half-light of the moon. The leaves of the corn rustled gently with every faint breeze, and here and there in the distance a dog barked, and high in the heavens above, the glittering lights of the Milky Way winked. I felt overcome then by a grand serenity.

Or consider the town in which I now live, a modest rural village born in the hard times of the 1870s when locusts swarmed over the newly broken prairies by the billions, devouring the hopes of the settlers. It has no scenic vista, no grand edifices. It has never been notably prosperous. These days there are three main approaches to it. Along one of them the interstate highway runs and has given birth to a neon strip of fast food joints and discount houses. Along the second are situated the settling ponds for the packing plant, ripe with the odor of decay. Along the third is located one of the largest farm equipment salvage yards in the nation, acres of rusting tractors and combines. No casual visitor to the town could possibly think on first impression that it was picturesque. I myself, I suppose, would never have come to it had I not taken a job there sight unseen.

But I have lived here for a dozen years now, and I take constant pleasure in its beauties. It is not that I don't see its uglinesses or that I don't despair now and then at the complacencies that make them tolerable. I do and I do. But it is also a place in which I have made wonderful friendships, and friendships have a way of beautifying a landscape. And I know, within its corporate limits, where to catch a bass or a sunfish, where the beaver lives, where the orioles make their nests. I have seen the ducks and geese flock to its prairie lake by the thousands. I have seen the wild mink and the white-faced opossum wandering its streets by lamplight. I have watched gardens bloom and snows fall as white as egrets. There I have seen suns set and moons rise, and heard the doves cooing in the mornings and the crows cawing in the crisp evenings of September. The more familiar it has become to me, the more I have learned to love it, and the more I have loved it, the more beautiful it has seemed.

Minnesota, certainly, is possessed of many classically beautiful places. The canoe country of the north is such a place, that wild maze of rocks and clear, cold waters and tall pines in which the wolves and the loons make their last stand. The rolling moraines of west central Minnesota, dotted with aspens and oaks, are such a place. Lake Superior's North Shore with its great cliffs and its sea roar is such a place. The tumbling St. Croix and the grand Mississippi—compared by early travelers with the Rhine—are such places. The rugged hills of southeastern Minnesota covered with hardwood forest and harboring trout streams and picturesque farms are such a place. Even the great pits left after the ore has been extracted on the Iron Range have the shocking beauty of their rust-red depths.

And there are many other places that would be counted beautiful if they were better known: the quartzite outcroppings of southwestern Minnesota, the granite outcroppings of the upper Minnesota River valley, the bottomlands of the Mississippi River and of the lower Minnesota River, the great prairie marshes, even in their present despoliation. I suppose no place is a less likely candidate for designation as scenic than the Red River Valley, which is so flat, my friend who lives there claims, that when he stands on his porch he has climbed high enough to see across North Dakota and half of Montana to the Rocky Mountains. But some of Minnesota's most spectacular prairie remnants are to be found there, and I cherish the memory of a cross-country ski outing along the Red River one moonlit January night when the limb of every tree carried a shawl of new snow and every crystal of snow sparkled like a baby-blue jewel.

We are proud of our lakes and we are beginning to love our north woods to death. The richness of our landscapes has made us a distinctively outdoors people. There are places in Minnesota where the fishing opener and the first weekend of the deer season are religious occasions; the state issues every year almost as many boat licenses as it has citizens; and a

A sledding silhouette   ANNIE GRIFFITHS BELT

tenth of all the registered visits to designated wilderness areas in the United States are made to the Boundary Waters Canoe Area, not because there are so many out-of-state visitors, but because Minnesotans travel ritualistically into the wilderness. Love of the out-of-doors is a part of the culture to which we are born.

But it is not, I think, the natural beauties of the Minnesota landscape that we most strongly identify with. A true Minnesotan's real joy is in the state's harshness, in the extremes of its weather, in the violence of its storms, in the viciousness of its mosquitoes. It is true! we say. It is quite impossible to live here! My family is in the habit of vacationing in the wintertime on the Pacific coast of Mexico. "Where are you from?" we are asked. "Minnesota," we say. "Minnesota!" every Mexican invariably says, eyes widening, never missing a beat. "In Minnesota it is very cold." "Si," we say proudly, "es muy fria." I happen to be writing this in Mexico, and I have just had exactly this conversation with the attendant at the Pemex station. I did not tell the truth. I did not say, "Actually, it was 72 degrees and the sun was shining brilliantly when we left Minnesota." I did not tell the truth because I am a loyal Minnesotan, flattered by its reputation and loath to besmirch it with mere facts.

In truth, the reputation is not entirely undeserved. The geographer John Borchert, in his study of the Upper Midwest, the region centering economically on Minneapolis-St. Paul, compares weather statistics for our region with those for Siberia and concludes that by the measure of extremes, at least, we do live in the equivalent of Siberia. I cannot imagine what can be so awful about Siberian exile.

If people from elsewhere know anything at all about Minnesota, they are likely to think it is cold, that it is somewhat unsettled, that it has wolves, and that it is populated by shy and inexpressive Norwegians, quite a few of them bachelor farmers. Minnesota's European heritage is actually more German than Nordic, although even many Minnesotans would be surprised to hear it.

One of the ways to characterize a place is to identify the targets of its jokes. In Minnesota, the jokes are about Norwegians, and none of them are worth printing, although most of them *have* been printed, and not only printed but collected and published between book covers, whereupon they always become regional best sellers, Norwegians being the biggest buyers. Ours is the only state I know of that has made a major industry out of jokes about how it has no sense of humor. When Garrison Keillor tells stories about Norwegian bachelor farmers, it is not so much, I suspect, because he actually knows any as because he is a Minnesotan, and this is a form of storytelling that Minnesotans practice instinctively, like breathing, from birth. In Minnesota all you need to do to get a laugh—or at least a good-humored groan—is to stand up and say, "Ole and Lena." Every member of the audience knows a hundred ways to finish the story, all of them, it is thought, hilarious.

The other things we joke about, because they are true, are our cooking and our conversations. Both suffer from an extravagant blandness. It is quite possible to get a meal in Minnesota in which every dish except the Jell-O is white and has been sauced with either condensed cream of mushroom soup or artificial whipped topping, and to have it followed by a conversation in which the most freewheeling remark is, "Ya well, I suppose a fella can't complain then."

We have our reformers who would like to get us all involved in group therapy with social workers from The Cities who could teach us how to get in touch with our emotions, and how to announce them to other folks, but obviously these people have never tried to imagine what life in the confines of a small town would be like if we made it a practice to say all the time exactly what was on our minds.

My wife and I were mildly unnerved the day we first moved to a little house in the country to find that although we hadn't yet formally notified the post office of our move, the first day's mail was already in the unlabeled roadside box when we arrived, and our nearest neighbors, whom we had not met, came by and greeted us warmly by name, as if we were old friends. Living successfully with strangers at this level of intimacy requires a certain discretion of speech. One does not always volunteer all that one knows or thinks. On the other hand, we locked the house up tight that first year when we left on vacation, and when we returned, we found that the keys we had been given were merely a ceremonial formality bearing no actual relation to the locks on the doors. We had to take the front door out of its frame to get back in. We learned then that there are certain pleasant securities in a world where everyone

A military history drill at Big Island Rendezvous, Helmer Myre State Park   GREG L. RYAN/SALLY A. BEYER

discreetly minds everyone else's business.

Beyond this, it is difficult to generalize about Minnesota, as about any place. I suppose it is striking to many visitors how homogeneous the state's population is—something it has in common with many parts of the northern interior of our continent—but it remains homogeneous only in the European sense: many of its towns are still recognizably Dutch or French or Polish or German or Finnish. It has river towns and farming towns, mining towns and resort towns, reservation towns and bedroom towns, port towns and industrial towns. It has a booming strip metropolis and, along its western border, ghost towns. It serves as headwaters to the nation's greatest river, and the waters of the world's largest lake form one of its shores. Although it lies at the heart of the continent, it is connected by water with the Atlantic Ocean, the Gulf of Mexico, and Hudson's Bay. At the headwaters of the Mississippi three great temperate zone ecosystems meet: the grasslands, the northern coniferous forest, and the eastern deciduous forest. It stretches far enough north to host an occasional caribou, far enough south to harbor rattlesnakes. It knows arctic cold and tropical heat. There are places deep in its northern bogs that no human may ever have set foot upon in modern times, and there are vast stretches of its prairies that have been wholly remade into human gardens in the last century. I was carried home as an infant to a house without electricity or plumbing, but I lived only a morning's drive from one of the great centers of high technology. It is mountainously rugged, as I can attest from having walked its northeastern border with Ontario, and it is breathtakingly flat. In its reach and diversity, it is as little insular as any place on the continent.

Once in Zurich I met a man whose wisdom was positively Minnesotan. "My friend," he said, "he moved to Arizona—do you know him, his name is___—and he writes to me and says, 'Really, you must come to America. You wouldn't believe it. It is so *big*!' But I say to him, 'You know, when I go walking in Switzerland it seems big enough for me.'"

There are other great and beautiful places in the world, but when I go walking in Minnesota, as I often do, it, too, seems to me great enough and sufficiently beautiful. For this lifetime, at least, it will be entirely sufficient.

Paul Gruchow
Worthington, Minnesota

A commanding view of Duluth and Lake Superior from Skyline Drive   KEN DEQUAINE/THIRD COAST STOCK SOURCE

> *I have spent forty of my sixty years outside of Minnesota—on the Atlantic seaboard, in California, in Europe. But I wonder, unendingly, whether I might not have been a much better writer had I spent all my life, except a year or two in the East, for contrast, in my native Minnesota. Like Grant Wood and Thomas Benton and John Curry, I certainly find the prairies quite as productive of 'art' as any boulevard, any Massachusetts hillside.*

Sinclair Lewis,
Minnesota Writers

Whitetail doe   DANIEL J. COX

Bloodroot   D. CAVAGNARO

A pond in northern Minnesota CRAIG BLACKLOCK

Portage River in the Boundary Waters Canoe Area   DAVID MUENCH

Kabetogama Lake in Voyageurs National Park   JEFF GNASS

The state capitol dome and St. Paul Cathedral in St. Paul   GREG L. RYAN/SALLY A. BEYER

A rainbow over downtown Minneapolis   CHUCK KEELER/FROZEN IMAGES

Low clouds over the Boundary Waters Canoe Area ANNIE GRIFFITHS BELT

" *And the fog lay on the river,*
Like a ghost, that goes at sunrise. . . . "

Henry Wadsworth Longfellow,
The Song of Hiawatha

Dawn breaking over a northern forest   ANNIE GRIFFITHS BELT

Wild geranium   JOHN SHAW

Downy phlox and Canada anemones on Wahpeton Prairie   CARL KURTZ

A common loon, the Minnesota state bird, on its nest   DANIEL J. COX

A loon in a mating display   DANIEL J. COX

❝ *Above came a swift whisper of wings, and as the loons saw us they called wildly in alarm, increased the speed of their flight, and took their laughing with them into the gathering dusk. Then came the answers we had been waiting for, and the shores echoed and re-echoed until they seemed to throb with the music. This was the symbol of the lake country, the sound that more than any other typifies the rocks and waters and forests of the wilderness.* ❞

Sigurd F. Olson,
Listening Point

The shoreline of Clearwater Lake in the Boundary Waters Canoe Area   CHUCK KEELER/FROZEN IMAGES

Black bear   DANIEL J. COX

Some years later I discovered a stand of virgin forest known as the Northwest Corner. Here were tremendous trees, the last of the old primeval stand, and on the ground huge moss-covered logs soft and spongy with decay. . . . I used to tiptoe into the timber and creep stealthily from bole to bole, thrilled with strange and indefinable sensations, some of fear and some of wonder and delight. Those ancient trees, the green-gold twilight among them, the silence of that cushioned place did something to my boyish soul which I have never forgotten.

Sigurd F. Olson,
Minnesota Writers

Mushrooms along the Lake Superior Hiking Trail   GREG L. RYAN/SALLY A. BEYER

Cascade Falls State Park   DAVID MUENCH

Ice along Lake Superior   T. RUMREICH/FROZEN IMAGES

> **If there were snows to remember, there were the dazzling nights when your breath crisped inside your nostrils and the moon had blazing rings around it. Such clear nights that the stars sprang up at the edges of the pasture. And the Northern Lights spangled in silent fireworks all across the sky. Those cold clear nights so still that if you sang while carrying firewood, the man three farms away could hear you and yodel back.** "

Shirley Schoonover,
"Route 1, Box 111, Aurora,"
Growing Up in Minnesota

Branches locked in ice   BOB FIRTH

Taking a break from snowshoeing   ANNIE GRIFFITHS BELT

  The fact is that most country or small-town Minnesotans love snow. They relish snow in large inconvenient storms; they like the excesses of it, they like the threat of it, the endless work of it, the glamour of it. **"**

Carol Bly,
Letters from the Country

Early winter on the Cascade River GREG L. RYAN/SALLY A. BEYER

Sunrise on the Whiteface River   DANIEL J. COX

" The sun had no strength these days. It peeped out in the morning, glided across the sky as before, yet life it had not until toward evening, as it was nearing the western rim of the prairie. Then it awoke, grew big and blushing, took on a splendour which forced everyone to stop and look; the western sky foamed and flooded with a wanton richness of colour, which ran up in streams to meet the coming night. "

O. E. Rölvaag,
Giants in the Earth

A fisherman's sunset   MITCH KEZAR/FROZEN IMAGES

> **"** *The aspen, the birch, and the maples colored almost overnight, but the oaks, conservative to the end, slowly turned to deep and shining red and finally to a waxy, gleaming mahogany. But when the storms came out of the north and the brilliant ones stood stripped and bare, they were fully clothed and far more beautiful than the rest had ever been because they stood alone.* **"**

Sigurd F. Olson,
The Singing Wilderness

Birch and maple trees in Voyageurs National Park DAVID MUENC

Grasses and red sumac at Pipestone National Monument DAVID MUENCH

Autumn leaves at Jay Cooke State Park   GREG L. RYAN/SALLY A. BEYER

A fall-colored forest near the north shore of Lake Superior   ANNIE GRIFFITHS BELT

" And then, in the hush of the forest, perhaps while you are toiling along some portage path, you will hear from a distant thicket a hymn never meant for mortal ears. No trace of earth in the hermit thrush's sublime matins and vespers—only the ecstasy of serene faith. "

Grace Lee Nute,
The Voyageur's Highway: Minnesota's Border Lake Land

Maple leaves   ROBERT M. FRIEDMAN/FROZEN IMAGES

A farm near Afton   GREG L. RYAN/SALLY A. BEYER

“ *South, in the farming country, there are four seasons. The farmer invented them, and they are for planting, for growing, for harvesting, and for resting. But in the North there are only two seasons, the open and the closed seasons. Spring is a moment at the time of breakup; the unwary will miss it completely, and find summer on him, unannounced. Fall begins in the last week of August, when a single confused maple turns red on the shore.* ”

John Szarkowski,
The Face of Minnesota

A bumper harvest of pumpkins   GREG L. RYAN/SALLY A. BEYER

Moss covering a forest floor GLENN VAN NIMWEGEN

A stand of paper birch along the north shore of Lake Superior MICHAEL MAGNUSON

Log-rolling at the Minnesota State Fair   STEVEN G. RUEHLE

❝ Minnesotans are just different, that's all. On the day of which I speak, with the wind-chill factor hovering at fifty-seven below, hundreds of them could be perceived through the slits in my ski mask out ice fishing on this frozen lake. It was cold out there, bitter, biting, cutting, piercing, hyperborean, marmoreal cold, and there were all these Minnesotans running around outdoors, happy as lambs in the spring. ❞

Charles Kuralt,
Dateline America

An informal game of ice hockey   BOB FIRTH

Ice fishing for perch   DANIEL J. COX

Speed skaters at the St. Paul Winter Carnival   STEVE SCHNEIDER

A cross-country skier training with roller skis KURT MITCHELL/FROZEN IMAGES

Minnesota honoring its Twins, 1987 World Series champions MIKE MAGNUSON

The Minnesota Vikings in the Hubert H. Humphrey Metrodome STEVE SCHNEIDER

Making waves   BOB FIRTH

Triathlon swimmers hit the water
ROBERT M. FRIEDMAN/FROZEN IMAGES

The House of Representatives chamber in St. Paul   BOB FIRTH

Piper Jaffray Tower in Minneapolis   SCENIC PHOTO IMAGERY

Indian regalia at Grand Portage BOB FIRTH

" *I think people, people tend to be the voice of the land . . . every soil develops a voice through its people.* "

Frederick Manfred,
Fiction

Winter fun-lovers near St. Mary's Catholic Church, New Trier   GREG L. RYAN/SALLY A. BEYER

"" *The winter sky is the plain and homely sister of the skies, the sad-sack one, the ash sky, all gray and featureless, pale in the morning, pale at noon, pale at night.* ""

Paul Gruchow,
Journal of a Prairie Year

Palisade Head from Baptism River State Park, Lake Superior   TOM ALGIRE

A solar halo and sundogs   JIM BRANDENBURG/FROZEN IMAGES

" ** *The winter sky does, however, have its moments. They are the moments at dusk or at dawn when the angle of the light is exactly right to catch the crystalline haze in the air. Then the sun can be seen to be crowned with a halo or bracketed by sun dogs, and sometimes these dogs are as brilliantly multicolored as the rainbows that follow the summer rains. Or the sun seems just at the moment of setting to take the shape of a Roman cross, belled at the bottom and luminescent. It is on such nights that the lights of the little prairie towns stretch up into the sky like searchlights. Every settlement seems surrounded then by its private show of Northern Lights.* **"

Paul Gruchow,
Journal of a Prairie Year

Otters   LES BLACKLOCK

" The silence of those miles of snow untouched by any trace of human beings, marked only by the inhuman winds and the paws of wild animals, was without enmity or pity. "

Rose Wilder Lane,
Let the Hurricane Roar

Wolverine ANNIE GRIFFITHS BELT

Gray wolf DANIEL J. COX

Great blue heron   JOHN AND ANN MAHAN

Headwaters of the Mississippi River, Itasca State Park   GREG L. RYAN/SALLY A. BEYER

A fly fisherman's dream   GREG L. RYAN/SALLY A. BEYER

❝ *Gone are the snows of winter. The creeks are running. The birds are back. Nature has come alive.* **❞**

Irid Bjerk,
Boy off the Farm

The Mississippi River near its source   CARL KURTZ

Lake Superior pummeling its shoreline during a storm   ANNIE GRIFFITHS BELT

" . . .the great pine trunks were gilded with light, and ferns and mats of blueberries were enameled mosaics, gold, green-gold, and green-blue. There was a breath of scented wind, and then we heard a hermit thrush singing, the first one we have heard in our canoe country. That most haunting gold-dark song, golden with realized rapture, dark with unrealized grief—I shall never hear it again without longing for this place. "

Florence Page Jaques,
Canoe Country

Paddling through morning mist   R. HAMILTON SMITH/FROZEN IMAGES

    " Autumn meant days filled with warmth and softened sunshine; nights cool and frosty, with white mists swirling and running over the lakes in the mornings; portage paths carpets of red and gold, filled with the smell of leaves. It meant grasses, ferns, and weeds varying in color from sienna to bronze and copper; green pine forests tinted with the gold leaves of aspen and birch and the fire of maple; blueberry, honeysuckle, poison ivy, sumac, and Juneberry—all vivid shades of scarlet and gold. "

J. Arnold Bolz,
Portage into the Past

Kabetogama Lake, Voyageurs National Park   TOM TILL

" The sun hovered in its descent, its glow reflected in the incandescence of the clouds. When it dropped from sight, the clouds blazed red, then subsided in a radiant flush of rose. The lake glistened in reflected glory and the forest was bathed in a champagne haze that erupted over the pines in a halo of flame. "

J. Arnold Bolz,
Portage into the Past

Sunrise over Lake Calhoun CARL KURTZ

> *When last I was there waving fields of grain greeted my eye, and green pastures, and a happy, industrious people who joyfully turned to account the rich harvest with which the state had been blessed.* **99**

Hugo Nisbeth,
Selections from Minnesota History

Picking wild raspberries   DANIEL J. COX

The juicy harvest   DANIEL J. COX

Ready for picking at an apple orchard in Stillwater   GREG L. RYAN/SALLY A. BEYER

Stacking hay in southern Minnesota   ANNIE GRIFFITHS BELT

Farming   ANNIE GRIFFITHS BELT

Feeding a friend   GREG L. RYAN/SALLY A. BEYER

" *I loved the farm, with its wooded river and creek banks, its tillage and crops, and its cattle and horses.* **"**

Charles A. Lindbergh,
Autobiography of Values

Cliffs at Blue Mounds State Park   CRAIG BLACKLOCK

The mounds are a mesa, a table. Ice carved the table out of the Sioux quartzite bedrock. Its edge is a two-mile-long line of sheer cliffs a hundred feet high, split in many places by the ravages of weather, pulled apart by the muscular forces of roots, rent by deep, narrow canyons. It is a vast ruin, all tumbles of talus and crumbling chimney spires.

Paul Gruchow,
The Necessity of Empty Places

Quartzite at Blue Mounds State Park   DAVID MUENCH

Sunrise at Silver Island Lake in Superior National Forest   T. RUMREICH/FROZEN IMAGES

Sunrise over an island on Kabetogama Lake   GREG L. RYAN/SALLY A. BEYER

And the evening sun descending
Set the clouds on fire with redness,
Burned the broad sky, like a prairie,
Left upon the level water
One long track and trail of splendor. . . .

Henry Wadsworth Longfellow,
The Song of Hiawatha

Pink lady slipper   D. CAVAGNARO

Maple leaves at their fiery best   WALLY EBERHART

Autumn at Oberg Mountain, near the north shore of Lake Superior   CRAIG BLACKLOCK

Enjoying the land of sky-blue waters   PETER HECK/FROZEN IMAGES

Costumed interpreters' helpers at historic Fort Snelling in Minneapolis   GREG L. RYAN/SALLY A. BEYER

A worker at the 3M plant in St. Paul   ANNIE GRIFFITHS BELT

Products of the north woods   TOM TRACY/PHOTOGRAPHIC RESOURCES

Tugboat work at Duluth   JERRY BIELICKI

Paul Bunyan and Babe, Minnesota "natives"   BOB FIRTH

Crafting fish lures in Cambridge   GREG L. RYAN/SALLY A. BEYER

A monument to miners at Iron World, Chisholm
SCENIC PHOTO IMAGERY

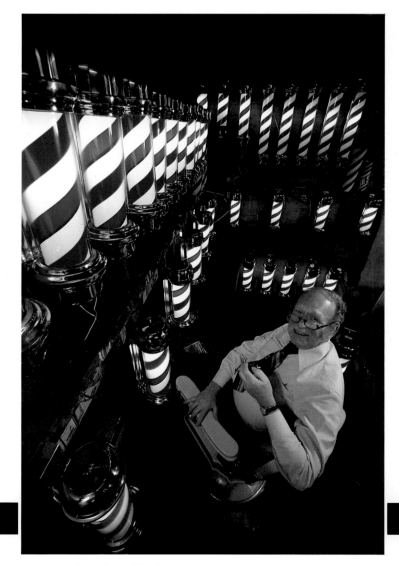

A maker of barber poles   ANNIE GRIFFITHS BELT

An evening snowstorm in Excelsior   MIKE MAGNUSON

Sled dog racing   ANNIE GRIFFITHS BELT

Ready for a sleigh ride   GREG L. RYAN/SALLY A. BEYER

Waiting for spring   ANNIE GRIFFITHS BELT

Smelting in the Lester River   DANIEL J. COX

A commercial smelt catch   DANIEL J. COX

Como Park Conservatory in St. Paul   SCENIC PHOTO IMAGERY

Ice climbing on a frozen waterfall BOB FIRTH

The Mississippi River in its youth   GLENN VAN NIMWEGEN

" The broad valley, the swiftly moving water and verdant islands and banks, are not so greatly changed from the time of early explorers, and there remain places along the river where there is no sound other than that of flowing water or leaves moving in a summer breeze. "

William E. Lass,
Minnesota—A History

Brown-eyed susans and fleabane daisies   MICHAEL MAGNUSON

A paddlewheel boat carrying tourists on the Mississippi   ANNIE GRIFFITHS BELT

Early morning dew, Blue Mounds State Park   GREG L. RYAN/SALLY A. BEYER

Plying sun-drenched waters   ROBERT A. FRIEDMAN/FROZEN IMAGES

The thrilling cadence of their wild honking cries rose and fell in rhythm with their heavy, powerful surge through the warm autumn air. As they passed with necks outstretched, low over the canoe, the sun revealed white patches on the sides of their black heads and highlighted the beat of their wings. Their crying softened and died as they vanished into the southern sky.

J. Arnold Bolz,
Portage into the Past

Canada goose   ROB SHEPPARD/FROZEN IMAGES

Spleenwort fern surrounded by blue phlox   D. CAVAGNARO

❝ This wilderness was an arena for feelings of intense and new delight. The sublime traits of nature; phenomena which fill the soul with astonishment, and inspire it at the same time with almost heavenly ecstasy! ❞

Giacomo Beltrami,
Early 19th century Minnesota explorer
quoted in Mark Twain's Mississippi

Water shield leaves   WALLY EBERHART

Sailing on Lake Minnetonka   ANNIE GRIFFITHS BELT

Lake Superior   RONALD MORREIM

High Bridge in St. Paul   BOB FIRTH

Farmers market in Minneapolis   ROBERT M. FRIEDMAN/FROZEN IMAGES

“ *That's pretty conservative country I come from. . . . We don't go in for these far-out things. We don't like far-out art or far-out politics.* ”

Hubert H. Humphrey,
quoted in The Drugstore Liberal

Sunrise over Lake Superior near Temperance River State Park   DAVID MUENCH

Fall colors reflected in Heyman Lake, Boundary Waters Canoe Area   DAVID MUENCH

" I don't know when I first knew I was in love with this sometimes harsh and demanding land. Did I fall in love in winter, when the snow is cold and crunchy as one pads along on snowshoes? . . . Or did I fall in love when the change from winter to spring begins, and one hears the sound of the first gentle rain on the roof, running off in rivulets? . . . I don't know when, but the fact remains that I did fall in love. An infinitesimal speck in the cosmos, I stood on the shore of Gunflint Lake beneath a great white pine—matriarch of a fast-vanishing tribe. And I knew I was home. "

Justine Kerfoot,
Woman of the Boundary Waters

Rusty Point, Lake Superior   TOM ALGIRE

Oats and rye   R. HAMILTON SMITH

> **" An endlessly breaking wave crests and falls behind me. When you drive down a country road and see windrowed hay lying out in the fields, it seems to cling to the stubble, to be a level disturbance of color. But when you rake it, the tines lift it up, pass it along to the right, and stand it on edge in a high line. The meaning of windrow—a row through which wind blows— becomes clear. "**

Verlyn Klinkenborg,
Making Hay

Aerial view of a Minnesota farm   R. HAMILTON SMITH

Down on the farm   BOB FIRTH

❝ *But a barn is also a cathedral where visiting townboys come to worship farm life. It has the well-rubbed wood of a reverenced church rail, the grain raised by the protruberant hides of quietly agnostic cows. In the hayloft you learn the meaning of motes and beams. You walk across its plank floor, head tilted back. Day outside finds cracks in the roof and walls of the hayloft, and light streaks through the darkness on missions of grace and accusation. The barn is wired to God's wrath by a lightning rod.* **❞**

Verlyn Klinkenborg,
Making Hay

Hay shed   BOB FIRTH

Glacial erratic, Voyageurs National Park   DAVID MUENCH

Moss on granite, Voyageurs National Park   DAVID MUENCH

American lotus lilies at Fort Snelling State Park   GREG L. RYAN/SALLY A. BEYER

66 Nature seems to have lavished all her treasures on this beautiful valley; watered by the river St. Peter, it possesses a fertile soil, a salubrious climate, hills and plains adapted to every sort of cultivation, rivers and lakes abounding in fish, shellfish and game, richest fur and furnishing every variety of timber for building . . . and added to all these riches, magnificent stone which might be worked with the greatest facility and fitted for building barns, houses, temples, palaces. . . . 99

Giacomo Beltrami,
Early 19th century Minnesota explorer
describing the Minnesota River Valley

Ferns and maple leaves along the St. Louis River   GREG L. RYAN/SALLY A. BEYER

After a storm near Victoria   MIKE MAGNUSON

Sunflowers   JAMES O. SNEDDON

Prairie chicken   CRAIG BLACKLOCK

Morning mist enveloping Kathio State Park   GREG L. RYAN/SALLY A. BEYER

The sun was trembling now on the edge of the ridge. It was alive, almost fluid and pulsating, and as I watched it sink I thought that I could feel the earth turning from it, actually feel its rotation.

Sigurd F. Olson,
The Singing Wilderness

Sunrise over the St. Croix River   CARL KURTZ

A grouse hunter and his best friend   DANIEL J. COX

❝ *If a man walk in the woods for love of them half of each day, he is in danger of being regarded as a loafer; but if he spends his whole day as a speculator, shearing off those woods and making earth bald before her time, he is esteemed an industrious and enterprising citizen.* **❞**

Henry David Thoreau,
Life without Principle

Strolling under a golden arch   STEVE SCHNEIDER

Whitetail buck   TOM AND PAT LEESON

> *When the whitetail shifts into high gear he surpasses any broken-field runner that football gridirons have ever known. The scent of danger causes the tail to raise in a flash of white. Then, with the 'flag' waving the deer is off to the races—a streamlined, soaring, running, leaping, darting beauty whose movements seem so typical of the wild and the free.*

Minnesota Department of Natural Resources

Whitetail buck   DANIEL J. COX

A country road   RONALD MORREIM

❝ *In the lakes, the prairie by moonlight, the wide wheat fields on July afternoons, the hysterical doings of Sunday School picnics and Christmas entertainments, the noble deeds of the high school in athletics . . . in the amiable mixture of Scandinavians and Bavarians and Yankees, in the shadow of the great North Woods that just dimly reached my town, I found inspiration more than enough.* **❞**

Sinclair Lewis,
Minnesota Writers

A glowing end to a backcountry day   ANNIE GRIFFITHS BELT

Canoe Country in northern Minnesota   DANIEL J. COX

> ❝ *I have got to have the sight of clean water and the sound of running water. I have got to get to places where the sky-shine of cities does not dim the stars, where you can smell land and foliage, grasses and marshes, forest duff and aromatic plants and hot underbrush turning cool. Most of all, I have to learn again what quiet is.* ❞

Bernard DeVoto,
Harper's

Gooseberry Falls, Gooseberry Falls State Park   GREG L. RYAN/SALLY A. BEYER

> *Came the Spring with all its splendor,*
> *All its birds and all its blossoms,*
> *All its flowers, leaves, and grasses.*

Henry Wadsworth Longfellow,
The Song of Hiawatha

Whitetail fawn   DANIEL J. COX

116

A child of the north woods   ANNIE GRIFFITHS BELT

Pink and white lady slippers   JOHN SHAW

they made it possible

Minnesota on my Mind would have been impossible to produce without the keen eyes and technical skills of more than thirty professional photographers. These men and women succeeded in a difficult task—capturing the many moods and faces of Minnesota. From sparkling city lights to shimmering backcountry lakes, Minnesota harbors an array of beautiful images, but transforming these images onto film requires more than just a camera. It takes an eye for composition, technical expertise, the willingness to work in all weather, and, perhaps most important, the extra effort and patience that often separates an extraordinary photograph from a mere snapshot.

The photographers for *Minnesota on my Mind* provided this extra effort, whether it was lying down in a soggy meadow to photograph a delicate wild orchid or focusing on the geometric lines of a farmer's field while being tossed around in a bumpy small plane.

To all the excellent photographers who contributed to *Minnesota on my Mind*, thank you.

Michael S. Sample and Bill Schneider
Publishers, Falcon® Publishing

Photographers in *Minnesota on my Mind*

Tom Algire
Peter Beck
Annie Griffiths Belt
Greg L. Ryan/Sally A. Beyer
Jerry Bielicki
Craig Blacklock
Les Blacklock
Jim Brandenburg
D. Cavagnaro
Daniel J. Cox
Ken Dequaine
Wally Eberhart
Bob Firth
Robert M. Friedman
Jeff Gnass
Chuck Keeler
Mitch Kezar
Carl Kurtz
Tom & Pat Leeson
Michael Magnuson

John & Ann Mahan
Kurt Mitchell
Ronald Morreim
David Muench
Glenn Van Nimwegen
Steven G. Ruehle
T. Rumreich
Steve Schneider
John Shaw
Rob Sheppard
Richard Hamilton Smith
James O. Sneddon
Tom Till
Tom Tracy
And these photo agencies:
    Frozen Images
    Photographic Resources
    Scenic Photo Imagery
    Third Coast Stock Source

acknowledgments

The publishers gratefully acknowledge the following sources:

Pages 8, 21, and 112 from *Minnesota Writers,* edited by Carmen Nelson Richards. Copyright © 1961 by T.S. Denison & Co., Inc.

Page 19 from *Listening Point* by Sigurd F. Olson. Copyright © 1958 by Sigurd F. Olson. Reprinted by permission of Alfred A. Knopf, Inc.

Page 24 from "Route 1, Box 111, Aurora" by Shirley Schoonover in *Growing Up in Minnesota* edited by Chester G. Anderson. Copyright © 1976 by the University of Minnesota. Reprinted by permission of the University of Minnesota Press.

Page 26 from *Letters from the Country* by Carol Bly. Copyright © 1981 by Carol Bly. Reprinted by permission of Harper & Row, Publishers, Inc.

Page 28 from *Giants in the Earth* by O.E. Rölvaag. Copyright © 1955 by Jennie Marie Berdahl Rölvaag. Reprinted by permission of Harper & Row, Publishers, Inc.

Pages 30 and 106 from *The Singing Wilderness* by Sigurd F. Olson. Copyright © 1956 by Sigurd F. Olson. Reprinted by permission of Alfred A. Knopf, Inc.

Page 34 quoted from Grace Lee Nute, *The Voyageur's Highway: Minnesota's Border Lake Land* (St. Paul: Minnesota Historical Society, 1941) page 95. Reprinted by permission of the Minnesota Historical Society.

Pages 36 and 77 from *The Face of Minnesota* by John Szarkowski. Copyright © 1958 by the University of Minnesota. Reprinted by permission of the University of Minnesota Press.

Page 40 from *Dateline America* by Charles Kuralt. Copyright © 1979 by CBS, Inc. Reprinted by permission of Harcourt Brace Jovanovich, Inc.

Pages 46 and 49 from *Journal of a Prairie Year* by Paul Gruchow. Copyright © 1985 by the University of Minnesota. Reprinted by permission of the University of Minnesota Press.

Page 50 from *Let the Hurricane Roar* by Rose Wilder Lane. Copyright © 1961 by Roger Lea MacBride.

Page 53 from *Boy off the Farm* by Irid Bjerk. Copyright © 1982 by the Center for Western Studies.

Page 55 from *Canoe Country* by Florence Page Jaques. Copyright © 1938 by the University of Minnesota. Reprinted by permission of the University of Minnesota Press.

Pages 57, 66 and 86 from *Portage into the Past* by J. Arnold Bolz. Copyright © 1960 by the University of Minnesota. Reprinted by permission of the University of Minnesota Press.

Page 60 from "A Swedish Visitor of the Early Seventies," in *Minnesota History,* edited and translated by Roy W. Swanson (December 1927). Reprinted by permission of the Minnesota Historical Society.

Page 63 from *Autobiography of Values* by Charles A. Lindbergh. Copyright © 1978 by Harcourt Brace Jovanovich, Inc., and Anne Morrow Lindbergh. Reprinted by permission of the publisher.

Page 64 from *The Necessity of Empty Places* by Paul Gruchow. Copyright © 1988 by Paul Gruchow. Reprinted by permission of St. Martin's Press, Inc., New York.

Page 82 from *Minnesota: A History* by William E. Lass. Copyright © 1983 by The American Association for State and Local History.

Page 92 from *The Drugstore Liberal* by Robert Sherrill and Harry W. Ernst. Copyright © 1968 by Robert Sherrill and Harry W. Ernst.

Page 94 from *Woman of the Boundary Waters* by Justine Kerfoot. Copyright © 1986 by Justine Kerfoot. Reprinted by permission of Women's Times Publishing.

Pages 96 and 98 from *Making Hay* by Verlyn Klinkenborg. Copyright © 1986 by Verlyn Klinkenborg. Reprinted by permission of Lyons & Burford, Publishers.

Page 102 from *Pine, Stream & Prairie* by James Gray. Copyright © 1945 by James Gray. Reprinted by permission of Alfred A. Knopf, Inc.

Page 110 from a conservation bulletin published by the Minnesota Department of Natural Resources. Reprinted by permission.

Page 114 from "The Easy Chair" by Bernard DeVoto. Copyright © 1955 by *Harper's Magazine.* All rights reserved. Reprinted from the September issue by special permission.

About Paul Gruchow

Minnesota author Paul Gruchow wrote the introduction to *Minnesota on my Mind.* Gruchow is a native Minnesotan, born and raised in Montevideo. He has been an editor for the *Minneapolis-St. Paul City Magazine,* the news and public affairs director for Minnesota Public Radio, and managing editor and co-owner of the *Worthington Daily Globe.* Gruchow's articles and columns have appeared in several magazines, including *Minnesota Monthly.* Gruchow has written one book about Minnesota, *Journal of a Prairie Year,* and another book about the Great Plains, *The Necessity of Empty Places.* He lives in Worthington.

A paddler's pause   R. HAMILTON SMITH